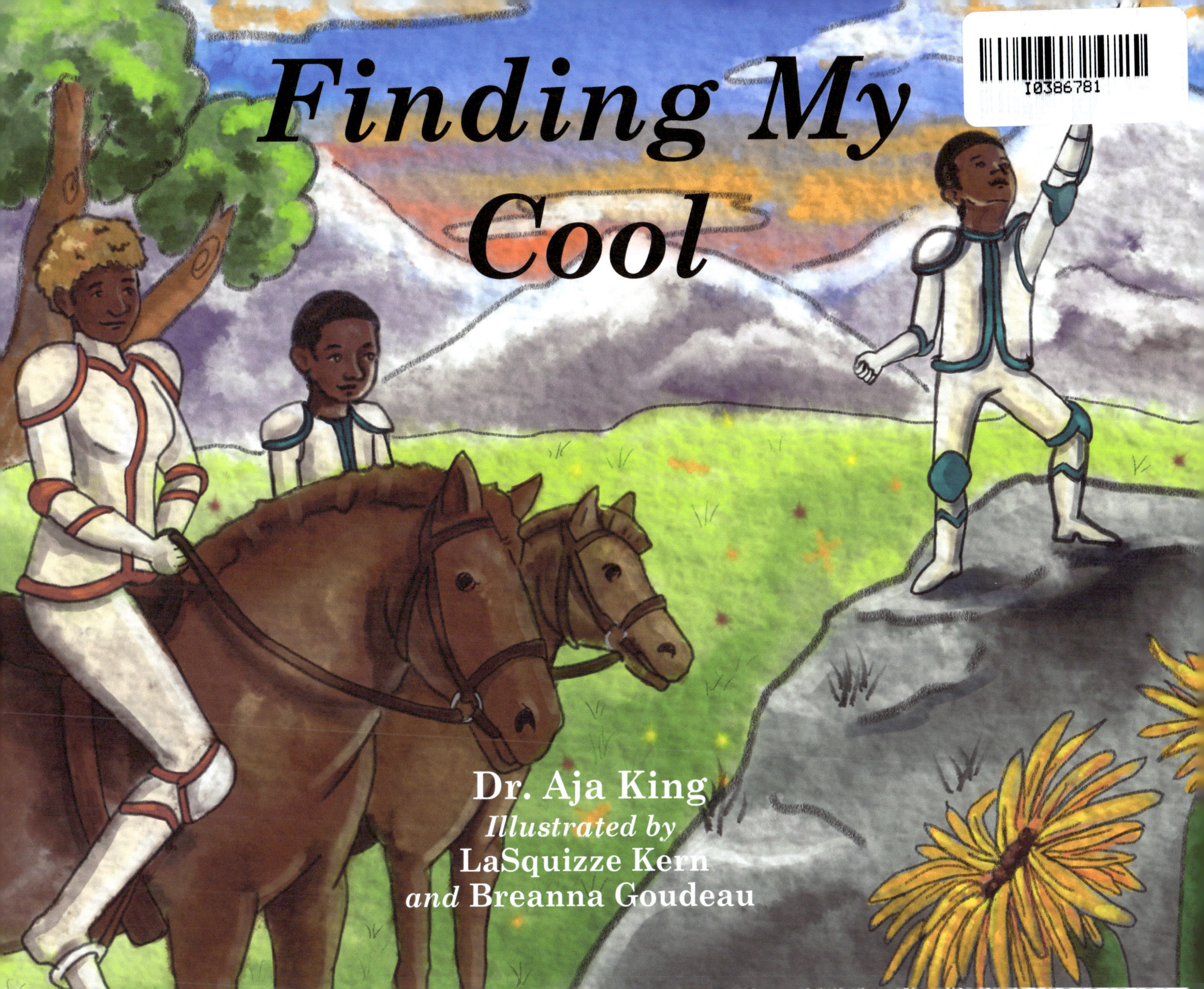

Copyright ©2019 Dr. Aja King

ISBN 978-0-578-48069-5 (Print)
ISBN 978-0-578-48070-1 (eBook)

All rights reserved. No part of this publication may be reproduced, distributed, or transmitted in any form or by any means, including photocopying, recording, or other electronic or mechanical methods, without the prior written permission of the publisher, except in the case of brief quotations embodied in critical reviews and certain other noncommercial uses permitted by copyright law.

Illustrated by LaSquizze Kern and Breanna Goudeau

Book design by StoriesToTellBooks.com

Who am I? Well, I'm Austin, and no adventure is too hard for this hero.

I've journeyed across the blistery snow to reach beautiful peaks.

I've even gathered my best comrades to travel the restless seas.

through all the adventures,

Finding my cool is not easy, and I hate when my feelings fall apart.

I lose most of my peace when I'm at school.

When I am angry, I cry until I fall asleep.

My mom says, "Austin, you need to find your peace."

My grandma and aunt say, "Sweetie, we love you and **know** you can do better."

Sometimes I wish
I could be like my brother, Chris.
He's always cool and hardly in trouble...

...especially at school.

Sometimes I wish I could be alone on an island with my favorite toys so I can always have my happiness.

But my mom says I can't leave because the world needs a hero, and so does she.

I like being me though!
You know why?

I'm **funny**,

brave, and <u>smart</u>!

Yet I still haven't found my cool.

I found my cool by releasing my *superhero energy*.

It's also when I stand like a *tree*.

Or when I **practice yoga** like a ninja.

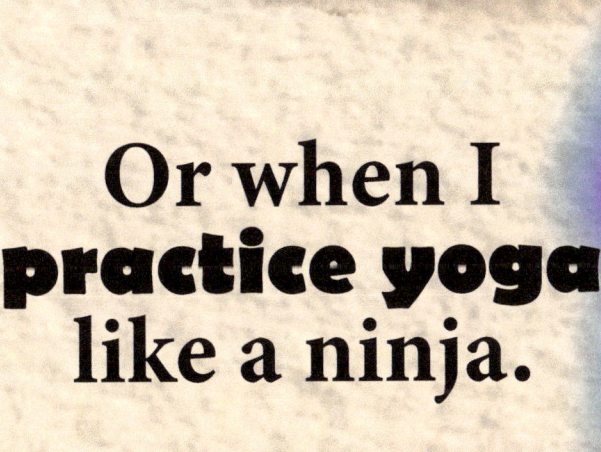

When I'm at school,

I sometimes take a break in my favorite calming space.

Being a kid can be tough and getting it right takes a bit more time.
Finding My Cool follows the journey of 7-year-old Austin and his family as they navigate his emotions in the world around him.
School, home, and hobbies are challenging, but Austin knows he has a destiny bigger than himself, and he is determined to find his COOL!

www.ingramcontent.com/pod-product-compliance
Lightning Source LLC
Chambersburg PA
CBHW040301100526

44584CB00004BA/295